Introduction

Welcome to "Freelancing with AI: How to Use AI Tools to Offer Writing, Editing, and Content Creation Services on Platforms Like Fiverr and Upwork." This book aims to empower freelancers with the knowledge and tools necessary to leverage artificial intelligence (AI) in their professional endeavors. Whether you are a seasoned freelancer or just starting, AI can revolutionize how you work, enhance the quality of your services, and significantly boost your productivity and income.

Introduction to Freelancing with AI

Overview of the Gig Economy

The gig economy has seen exponential growth over the past decade, driven by technological advancements and a shift in work culture. This new economy is characterized by temporary, flexible jobs where individuals work as independent contractors rather than traditional full-time employees. Popular platforms such as Fiverr, Upwork, and Freelancer.com have become hubs for freelancers offering various services, including writing, editing, graphic design, and more.

The appeal of the gig economy lies in its flexibility and the opportunity for individuals to work on projects that align with their skills and interests. Freelancers can choose their clients, set their rates, and define their work schedules. This autonomy attracts millions worldwide, seeking an alternative to the conventional 9-to-5 job structure.

The Role of AI in Transforming Freelancing

Artificial intelligence is no longer a futuristic concept; it is a transformative force reshaping industries, including freelancing. AI technologies are designed to mimic human intelligence, enabling machines to perform tasks such as understanding natural language, recognizing patterns, and making decisions.

For freelancers, AI offers many tools that can streamline workflows, enhance creativity, and improve service delivery. Here are a few ways AI is transforming freelancing:

1. **Automated Writing and Editing**: AI-powered tools like Jasper, Grammarly, and Copy.ai can generate high-quality content, suggest improvements, and correct errors, saving time and ensuring consistency.
2. **Content Creation**: AI can help create diverse content types, from blog posts and articles to social media updates and marketing materials, allowing freelancers to meet client demands quickly and efficiently.
3. **Market Analysis and Strategy**: AI tools can analyze market trends, consumer behavior, and competitor activities, providing valuable insights for freelancers to craft effective strategies and stay competitive.
4. **Project Management**: AI-driven project management tools can help freelancers organize tasks, set deadlines, and collaborate with clients, ensuring smooth project execution.

Benefits of Using AI for Freelancers

The integration of AI into freelancing brings numerous benefits, making it an indispensable asset for those looking to excel in the gig economy:

1. **Increased Efficiency**: AI automates repetitive tasks, freeing up time for freelancers to focus on more complex and creative aspects of their work. This increased efficiency translates to higher productivity and the ability to take on more projects.
2. **Enhanced Quality**: AI tools can help improve the quality of work by providing suggestions, detecting errors, and offering insights that might be missed by human eyes. This ensures that the final output meets high standards, leading to increased client satisfaction.
3. **Cost-Effective Solutions**: Many AI tools offer affordable solutions that can replace or supplement human labor, reducing operational costs for freelancers. This is particularly beneficial for those just starting and looking to minimize expenses.
4. **Competitive Edge**: Freelancers who leverage AI can deliver faster, more accurate, and more innovative services than their peers. This competitive edge can help attract more clients and build a robust freelance business.
5. **Scalability**: AI enables freelancers to scale their operations without compromising quality. By automating routine tasks, freelancers can handle more projects and expand their client base, leading to increased revenue potential.

In conclusion, AI is revolutionizing freelancing, providing tools and capabilities that were once unimaginable. By embracing these technologies, freelancers can enhance their services, improve efficiency, and gain a significant advantage in the ever-evolving gig economy. This book will guide you through the process of integrating AI into your freelancing business, offering practical tips and insights to help you succeed in this dynamic landscape.

Chapter 1: Understanding AI in Content Creation

Basics of AI

What is AI?

Artificial Intelligence (AI) refers to the development of computer systems capable of performing tasks that normally require human intelligence. These tasks include understanding natural language, recognizing patterns, solving problems, and making decisions. AI systems learn from data, improve over time, and can adapt to new information, making them incredibly versatile tools for a wide range of applications.

AI can be categorized into two types: narrow AI and general AI. Narrow AI, also known as weak AI, is designed to perform a specific task, such as language translation or image recognition. General AI, also known as strong AI, has the potential to understand, learn, and apply knowledge across various domains, similar to human intelligence. While general AI remains a theoretical concept, narrow AI is already being widely used in various industries, including content creation.

Types of AI Tools Available for Content Creation

AI tools for content creation are designed to assist with various stages of the writing and editing process. These tools can generate ideas, draft content, edit and proofread, and even optimize content for search engines. Here are some key types of AI tools available for content creation:

1. **Writing Assistants**: Tools like Jasper and Copy.ai can generate content based on given prompts, helping writers overcome writer's block and generate initial drafts quickly.
2. **Grammar and Style Checkers**: Tools like Grammarly and Hemingway analyze text for grammatical errors, style issues, and readability, providing suggestions for improvement.
3. **SEO Optimization Tools**: Tools like Clearscope and MarketMuse analyze content for SEO best practices, helping writers optimize their content for search engines.
4. **Content Ideation Tools**: Tools like BuzzSumo and AnswerThePublic generate content ideas based on trending topics and frequently asked questions, helping writers create relevant and engaging content.

5. **Plagiarism Checkers**: Tools like Copyscape and Turnitin compare text against a vast database of online content to ensure originality and avoid plagiarism.

AI in Writing and Editing

How AI Assists in Writing

AI-powered writing tools have revolutionized the content creation process by automating various aspects of writing. Here are some ways AI assists in writing:

1. **Idea Generation**: AI tools analyze trends, keywords, and user preferences to generate content ideas. For example, tools like BuzzSumo identify popular topics in your niche, while AnswerThePublic provides insights into common questions and search queries related to your topic.
2. **Drafting Content**: AI writing assistants like Jasper and Copy.ai can generate initial drafts based on given prompts. These tools use natural language processing (NLP) to understand the context and produce coherent and relevant content. This helps writers overcome writer's block and speeds up the drafting process.
3. **Content Structuring**: AI tools help organize content logically, ensuring a clear flow of ideas. For instance, Outwrite suggests improvements in sentence structure and paragraph organization, making the content more readable and engaging.
4. **Language Enhancement**: AI tools like Grammarly and Hemingway provide suggestions to enhance language, style, and tone. These tools analyze text for readability, conciseness, and engagement, ensuring the content resonates with the target audience.
5. **Personalization**: AI can tailor content to specific audiences by analyzing user data and preferences. Tools like Acrolinx ensure the content aligns with brand guidelines and audience expectations, making it more relevant and impactful.

AI Tools for Editing and Proofreading

Editing and proofreading are critical stages of the content creation process, ensuring that the final output is error-free, coherent, and polished. AI tools have significantly enhanced these stages by providing real-time feedback and suggestions. Here are some key AI tools for editing and proofreading:

1. **Grammar and Spelling Checkers**: Tools like Grammarly and Hemingway detect and correct grammatical errors, spelling mistakes, and punctuation

issues. They also provide suggestions for improving sentence structure and readability.
2. **Style Suggestions**: AI tools offer suggestions to improve writing style and tone. For example, Hemingway highlights complex sentences, passive voice, and adverbs, encouraging writers to simplify and strengthen their writing.
3. **Contextual Analysis**: Advanced AI tools analyze the context of sentences to provide more accurate corrections and suggestions. Tools like ProWritingAid offer in-depth analysis of writing style, readability, and consistency, helping writers refine their content.
4. **Plagiarism Detection**: AI-powered plagiarism checkers like Copyscape and Turnitin compare text against a vast database of sources to ensure originality. These tools help writers avoid unintentional plagiarism and maintain the integrity of their work.
5. **Tone Adjustment**: AI tools help adjust the tone of content to match the intended audience. For instance, Grammarly's tone detector analyzes the text and provides feedback on whether it sounds formal, friendly, or assertive, helping writers align their tone with their audience.
6. **Consistency Checking**: AI tools ensure consistency in terminology, formatting, and style throughout a document. Tools like PerfectIt check for consistency in capitalization, abbreviations, and numbers, ensuring a professional and polished final product.

In conclusion, AI has significantly transformed content creation by automating various aspects of writing and editing. By leveraging AI tools, freelancers can enhance their productivity, improve the quality of their work, and deliver exceptional content that meets the needs of their clients. As AI technology continues to evolve, the possibilities for innovation and efficiency in content creation are limitless.

Chapter 2: Setting Up Your Freelance Business

Choosing Your Niche

Identifying Profitable Niches

Choosing the right niche is crucial to your success as a freelancer. A profitable niche aligns with your skills, interests, and market demand. Here's a step-by-step guide to help you identify a lucrative niche:

1. **Research Market Demand**:
    a. **Analyze Trends**: Use tools like Google Trends, BuzzSumo, and SEMrush to identify trending topics and high-demand services in your field. Look for patterns in search volume, social media engagement, and content popularity.
    b. **Study Competitors**: Analyze the services offered by top freelancers on platforms like Fiverr and Upwork. Note which niches are saturated and which have a growing demand with fewer competitors.
    c. **Evaluate Job Listings**: Browse job postings on freelancing platforms to see what clients are looking for. Pay attention to the frequency of certain types of jobs and the rates being offered.
2. **Assess Profitability**:
    a. **Check Pricing**: Investigate how much clients are willing to pay for services in your potential niche. Compare the rates for different niches to see which offer higher earning potential.
    b. **Consider Long-Term Demand**: Choose niches that are not only trending now but have the potential for sustained demand. For example, AI-related services, digital marketing, and e-commerce support are likely to remain in demand.
3. **Evaluate Your Passion and Skills**:
    a. **Align with Interests**: Choose a niche that genuinely interests you. Passion for your work will drive your motivation and creativity, leading to higher quality services.
    b. **Leverage Your Expertise**: Assess your skills and experience. Choose a niche where you can confidently deliver high-quality work. For instance, if you have a background in marketing, consider niches like AI-powered marketing or content creation.

Matching Your Skills with Market Demand

Once you have identified profitable niches, it's essential to match your skills with market demand to ensure a good fit. Here's how you can do that:

1. **Conduct a Skills Inventory**:
    a. **List Your Skills**: Write down all your skills, including technical abilities, soft skills, and any specialized knowledge. Consider both hard skills (e.g., programming, writing) and soft skills (e.g., communication, project management).
    b. **Identify Transferable Skills**: Highlight skills that are transferable across different niches. For example, strong writing skills can be applied to content creation, copywriting, and editing services.
2. **Analyze Skill Gaps**:
    a. **Compare Skills with Niche Requirements**: Look at the skills required for the niches you are interested in. Identify any gaps in your skill set that need to be addressed.
    b. **Plan Skill Development**: Invest in learning new skills or improving existing ones. Online courses, webinars, and tutorials can help you acquire the necessary expertise. Platforms like Coursera, Udemy, and LinkedIn Learning offer courses on AI, digital marketing, and content creation.
3. **Test Your Skills in the Market**:
    a. **Start with Small Projects**: Take on smaller projects or offer your services at a discounted rate to build experience and gather feedback. This will help you refine your skills and understand client expectations.
    b. **Seek Feedback**: Request feedback from clients to identify areas for improvement. Use this feedback to enhance your services and better align with market demand.

Creating Your Portfolio

Showcasing AI-Enhanced Work

A strong portfolio is essential for attracting clients and showcasing your expertise. Here's how to create a compelling portfolio that highlights your AI-enhanced work:

1. **Select Your Best Work**:
    a. **Curate Quality Projects**: Choose a selection of your best work that demonstrates your skills and the value you can provide. Focus on quality over quantity.

    b. **Highlight AI Integration**: Include projects where you have successfully integrated AI tools. Explain how AI enhanced the final output, improved efficiency, or solved specific problems.
2. **Provide Detailed Case Studies**:
    a. **Describe the Project**: For each portfolio piece, provide a detailed description of the project, including the client's requirements, your approach, and the tools used.
    b. **Show Before and After**: If possible, include before-and-after examples to illustrate the impact of AI on the project. This can be particularly effective in showing the improvement in quality and efficiency.
    c. **Share Results**: Highlight the results achieved, such as increased engagement, higher conversion rates, or improved readability. Use metrics and testimonials to validate your success.
3. **Use Visuals**:
    a. **Incorporate Screenshots and Graphics**: Use visuals to make your portfolio more engaging and to provide a clear understanding of your work. Include screenshots of AI tools in action, content drafts, and final versions.
    b. **Create a Video Portfolio**: Consider creating a video portfolio that walks potential clients through your projects, explaining your process and showcasing your results. Tools like Canva can help you create professional and visually appealing videos.

Building a Professional Online Presence

Your online presence is critical for attracting clients and establishing credibility. Here are steps to build a professional online presence:

1. **Create a Professional Website**:
    a. **Domain and Hosting**: Purchase a custom domain name and reliable hosting. A professional URL (e.g., yourname.com) enhances credibility.
    b. **Design and Usability**: Use a clean, professional design with intuitive navigation. Platforms like WordPress, Squarespace, and Wix offer customizable templates.
    c. **Portfolio Section**: Include a dedicated portfolio section showcasing your best work, case studies, and testimonials. Make it easy for visitors to view your projects and understand your expertise.
    d. **About Page**: Write a compelling page that highlights your background, skills, and passion for freelancing. Include a professional photo and a brief biography.

e. **Contact Information**: Provide clear contact information, including an email address and contact form, making it easy for potential clients to reach you.
2. **Optimize for SEO**:
   a. **Keyword Research**: Identify keywords relevant to your services and niche. Use tools like Google Keyword Planner and Ahrefs to find high-volume, low-competition keywords.
   b. **Content Strategy**: Create high-quality content around these keywords to attract organic traffic. Write blog posts, articles, and guides that provide value to your target audience and showcase your expertise.
   c. **On-Page SEO**: Optimize your website's on-page elements, including meta titles, descriptions, headers, and image alt texts, to improve search engine visibility.
3. **Leverage Social Media**:
   a. **Choose Platforms**: Identify the social media platforms most relevant to your target audience. LinkedIn, Twitter, and Instagram are popular choices for freelancers.
   b. **Consistent Branding**: Use consistent branding across all platforms, including your profile picture, bio, and cover images. Ensure your branding reflects your professionalism and niche expertise.
   c. **Content Sharing**: Regularly share content that showcases your expertise and provides value to your audience. This can include blog posts, case studies, industry news, and tips related to your niche.
   d. **Engage with Your Audience**: Actively engage with your audience by responding to comments, participating in discussions, and connecting with potential clients and industry professionals.
4. **Join Freelance Platforms**:
   a. **Complete Profiles**: Create comprehensive profiles on freelance platforms like Fiverr, Upwork, and Freelancer.com. Include a professional photo, detailed descriptions of your services, and examples of your work.
   b. **Client Reviews**: Request reviews and testimonials from clients to build credibility. Positive reviews can significantly impact your visibility and attractiveness to potential clients.
   c. **Regular Updates**: Keep your profiles up-to-date with your latest projects, skills, and achievements. Regular updates signal to clients that you are active and continuously improving your services.

By carefully choosing your niche, matching your skills with market demand, and creating a compelling portfolio, you can set a strong foundation for your freelance business. Building a professional online presence will further enhance your credibility and attract clients, setting you on the path to success in the gig economy.

Chapter 3: Essential AI Tools for Freelancers

Writing Tools

Overview of Top AI Writing Tools

1. **Jasper (formerly Jarvis):**
   a. **Description**: Jasper is an AI-powered writing assistant that helps generate high-quality content based on user prompts. It uses GPT-3 technology to produce human-like text, making it ideal for creating blog posts, marketing copy, social media content, and more.
   b. **Key Features**:
      i. Content generation based on specific topics or keywords.
      ii. Multiple writing templates for different content types.
      iii. Built-in SEO optimization to help improve search engine rankings.
2. **Grammarly**:
   a. **Description**: Grammarly is an AI-powered grammar and writing tool that helps improve writing by detecting grammatical errors, punctuation mistakes, and style issues. It offers real-time suggestions and corrections to enhance clarity and readability.
   b. **Key Features**:
      i. Grammar and spell check.
      ii. Style and tone suggestions.
      iii. Plagiarism detection.
      iv. Integration with web browsers, Microsoft Office, and Google Docs.
3. **Copy.ai**:
   a. **Description**: Copy.ai is an AI-driven content generation tool designed to help users create engaging marketing copy, product descriptions, emails, and more. It offers various templates and customization options to tailor content to specific needs.
   b. **Key Features**:
      i. Content generation for multiple formats (ads, social media, blogs).

ii. Idea generation and brainstorming assistance.
iii. Customizable templates and tone settings.

How to Use These Tools Effectively

1. **Jasper**:
   a. **Content Planning**: Use Jasper to brainstorm and outline content ideas. Input specific keywords or topics to generate a list of potential blog post titles or article outlines.
   b. **Drafting**: Utilize Jasper's content generation capabilities to create initial drafts quickly. Provide detailed prompts to ensure the generated content aligns with your vision.
   c. **Editing**: After generating content, review and refine the output to add your unique voice and ensure accuracy. Use Jasper's SEO features to optimize the content for search engines.
2. **Grammarly**:
   a. **Real-Time Writing Assistance**: Install the Grammarly browser extension to get real-time writing suggestions while composing emails, social media posts, or online documents.
   b. **Document Review**: Upload your drafts to Grammarly's platform for a comprehensive review. Address the suggested corrections and improvements to enhance clarity, coherence, and correctness.
   c. **Style and Tone Adjustment**: Use Grammarly's tone detector to ensure your writing matches the desired style and tone, whether formal, casual, or friendly.
3. **Copy.ai**:
   a. **Marketing Copy**: Use Copy.ai's templates to generate persuasive marketing copy for ads, product descriptions, and landing pages. Input relevant information and customize the output to fit your brand's voice.
   b. **Idea Generation**: Leverage Copy.ai's brainstorming tools to generate ideas for blog posts, social media campaigns, and other content types. Experiment with different prompts to explore various angles and topics.
   c. **Content Variation**: Create multiple variations of the same content to test different approaches and find the most effective version for your audience.

Editing and Proofreading Tools

Best AI Editing Tools

1. **ProWritingAid**:
    a. **Description**: ProWritingAid is a comprehensive AI-powered editing tool that offers grammar checking, style improvement suggestions, and in-depth writing reports. It helps writers enhance their content's readability and overall quality.
    b. **Key Features**:
        i. Grammar and style check.
        ii. In-depth writing analysis reports.
        iii. Integration with popular writing platforms like Scrivener and Microsoft Word.
2. **Hemingway Editor**:
    a. **Description**: Hemingway Editor is an AI tool designed to improve writing clarity and readability. It highlights complex sentences, passive voice, and adverbs, encouraging writers to simplify and strengthen their content.
    b. **Key Features**:
        i. Readability scoring.
        ii. Highlighting complex sentences and passive voice.
        iii. Suggestions for simplifying text.

Integrating These Tools into Your Workflow

1. **ProWritingAid**:
    a. **Initial Draft Review**: After completing your first draft, run it through ProWritingAid to identify and correct grammatical errors, style issues, and readability problems.
    b. **Detailed Analysis**: Use ProWritingAid's in-depth reports to analyze different aspects of your writing, such as sentence structure, overused words, and pacing. Incorporate the feedback to refine your content.
    c. **Final Polishing**: Before publishing or submitting your content, perform a final check with ProWritingAid to ensure it meets high standards of quality and professionalism.
2. **Hemingway Editor**:
    a. **Simplifying Complex Sentences**: Copy and paste your draft into Hemingway Editor to identify complex sentences and passive voice. Rewrite these sentences to improve clarity and engagement.
    b. **Enhancing Readability**: Pay attention to the readability score provided by Hemingway Editor. Aim for a lower grade level to ensure your content is accessible to a broader audience.

    c. **Iterative Improvements**: Continuously use Hemingway Editor during the editing process to iteratively enhance your writing. Focus on making your content more concise and direct.

Content Creation and Management Tools

AI Tools for Generating and Managing Content

1. **ContentBot**:
    a. **Description**: ContentBot is an AI-powered tool that helps generate content ideas, drafts, and even complete articles. It offers various templates and content styles to suit different needs.
    b. **Key Features**:
        i. Idea generation and brainstorming.
        ii. Content drafts for blogs, social media, and emails.
        iii. Customizable content styles and tones.
2. **Frase**:
    a. **Description**: Frase is an AI-driven content optimization tool that helps create SEO-friendly content. It analyzes top-performing articles for given keywords and provides suggestions to improve your content's search engine ranking.
    b. **Key Features**:
        i. Content research and analysis.
        ii. SEO optimization and keyword suggestions.
        iii. Content briefs and outlines.

Automating Repetitive Tasks

1. **Zapier**:
    a. **Description**: Zapier is an automation tool that connects different apps and services, allowing users to automate repetitive tasks and workflows without coding.
    b. **Key Features**:
        i. Automate data entry, social media posting, and email campaigns.
        ii. Connect multiple apps and create workflows (Zaps) to streamline processes.
        iii. Integration with over 3,000 apps and services.
2. **IFTTT (If This Then That)**:

a. **Description**: IFTTT is an automation tool that enables users to create custom workflows and automate tasks based on specific triggers and actions.
   b. **Key Features**:
      i. Create applets to automate tasks like social media posting, content sharing, and data synchronization.
      ii. Integration with various apps and smart devices.
      iii. Simple, user-friendly interface for creating automation rules.

Implementing Automation in Your Workflow

1. **Streamline Content Distribution**:
   a. **Social Media Scheduling**: Use tools like Zapier and IFTTT to automate the scheduling and posting of your content across different social media platforms. Set up workflows to share new blog posts, videos, or articles automatically.
   b. **Email Campaigns**: Automate your email marketing campaigns by integrating your email service provider with AI tools. Create workflows to send welcome emails, follow-ups, and newsletters based on user actions and triggers.
2. **Manage Content Projects**:
   a. **Content Calendar**: Use AI tools to automate the management of your content calendar. Set up reminders, deadlines, and notifications to keep your projects on track.
   b. **Task Automation**: Automate repetitive tasks like data entry, file organization, and content tagging. Use Zapier to create workflows that streamline your project management processes.
3. **Enhance Collaboration**:
   a. **Team Communication**: Integrate AI tools with your team communication platforms (e.g., Slack, Microsoft Teams) to automate notifications, updates, and task assignments.
   b. **Document Sharing**: Automate the sharing and updating of documents with cloud storage integrations. Use workflows to ensure team members always have access to the latest versions of important files.

By leveraging these AI tools and integrating them into your workflow, you can enhance your productivity, improve the quality of your work, and streamline your freelancing business. Embrace the power of AI to stay competitive and deliver exceptional value to your clients.

Chapter 4: Getting Started on Fiverr and Upwork

Setting Up Your Profiles

Creating Standout Profiles on Fiverr and Upwork

Your profile on freelancing platforms like Fiverr and Upwork is your digital storefront, and making a great first impression is crucial. Here's how to create standout profiles:

1. **Professional Headshot**:
   a. **Quality Matters**: Use a high-resolution, professional photo. Ensure you are well-groomed, smiling, and dressed appropriately. A clear, friendly image builds trust with potential clients.
   b. **Consistency**: Use the same photo across all platforms and social media for brand consistency.
2. **Compelling Bio**:
   a. **Introduce Yourself**: Start with a brief introduction that includes your name and a tagline summarizing your expertise. For example, "Hi, I'm Jane Doe, an AI-powered content creation specialist."
   b. **Highlight Skills**: Clearly state your skills and experience. Focus on your AI expertise and how it benefits clients. Mention any relevant certifications or training.
   c. **Client Focused**: Explain how your services can solve client problems. Use a friendly and professional tone, and avoid jargon.
3. **Showcase Your Experience**:
   a. **Detailed Work History**: Include previous work experience relevant to your niche. Highlight any notable projects or clients.
   b. **Portfolio Samples**: Upload samples of your work. Use case studies to illustrate how you've used AI to enhance content creation, marketing, etc.
   c. **Testimonials and Reviews**: If you have positive feedback from previous clients, include it in your profile to build credibility.
4. **Skills and Certifications**:
   a. **List Relevant Skills**: Ensure all your relevant skills are listed. Include both AI-related skills (e.g., machine learning, natural language processing) and general freelancing skills (e.g., project management, communication).

b. **Certifications and Training**: Add any certifications or courses completed related to AI and content creation.

Highlighting Your AI Expertise

1. **Specialized AI Services**:
   a. **Define Your Niche**: Clearly define the AI services you offer. Whether it's AI-powered content creation, editing, or SEO, be specific about your expertise.
   b. **Explain AI Benefits**: Describe how AI enhances your services. Highlight benefits like improved efficiency, higher quality, and innovative solutions.
2. **Technical Proficiency**:
   a. **Tools and Technologies**: List the AI tools and platforms you are proficient in (e.g., Jasper, Grammarly, Copy.ai). Explain how you use them to deliver superior results.
   b. **Case Studies and Examples**: Provide examples of projects where AI significantly improved outcomes. Include metrics and client feedback to support your claims.
3. **Continual Learning**:
   a. **Stay Updated**: Mention any ongoing learning or professional development in the AI field. This shows clients that you are committed to staying current with technology trends.

Optimizing Your Gig Listings

Writing Compelling Gig Descriptions

1. **Attention-Grabbing Title**:
   a. **Clear and Specific**: Use clear, specific titles that include relevant keywords. For example, "AI-Powered Blog Writing Service" or "AI-Enhanced SEO Content Creation."
   b. **Highlight Benefits**: Emphasize the unique selling points (USPs) of your service, such as speed, quality, and innovation.
2. **Detailed Description**:
   a. **Client-Centered**: Start with a brief introduction that addresses client needs and how your services solve their problems. Use a conversational tone.
   b. **Service Breakdown**: Provide a detailed breakdown of what your service includes. Be clear about deliverables, processes, and tools used.

c. **AI Integration**: Explain how AI is integrated into your service. Highlight the advantages of using AI, such as accuracy, efficiency, and cutting-edge solutions.
   d. **Call to Action**: End with a strong call to action, encouraging clients to contact you or place an order.
3. **Professional Presentation**:
   a. **Formatting**: Use bullet points, headings, and short paragraphs to make your description easy to read.
   b. **Visuals**: Include images, infographics, or videos demonstrating your services and results. Visual content can significantly enhance your gig's appeal.

Using Keywords to Attract Clients

1. **Keyword Research**:
   a. **Identify Keywords**: Use tools like Google Keyword Planner, Ahrefs, or SEMrush to identify relevant keywords and phrases that potential clients are searching for.
   b. **Long-Tail Keywords**: Focus on long-tail keywords that are specific to your niche, such as "AI-powered content writing" or "AI-based SEO services."
2. **Incorporate Keywords**:
   a. **Gig Title**: Include your primary keyword in the gig title for better visibility.
   b. **Description and Tags**: Naturally incorporate keywords into your gig description and tags. Avoid keyword stuffing; ensure your content remains readable and engaging.
   c. **Profile Bio**: Use relevant keywords in your profile bio to improve your profile's search ranking on the platform.

Pricing Your Services

Setting Competitive Rates

1. **Market Research**:
   a. **Analyze Competitors**: Look at what other freelancers in your niche are charging. Consider their experience level, service quality, and client feedback.
   b. **Platform Standards**: Understand the pricing standards of Fiverr and Upwork. Rates can vary significantly between platforms and niches.

2. **Value-Based Pricing**:
    a. **Assess Your Value**: Consider the value you bring to clients. If your AI expertise significantly enhances service quality or efficiency, you can justify higher rates.
    b. **Package Services**: Create different service packages (e.g., basic, standard, premium) to cater to various client budgets and needs. Each package should offer increasing value and complexity.
3. **Starting Rates**:
    a. **Competitive Entry**: When starting, set competitive rates to attract initial clients and build your portfolio. As you gain experience and positive reviews, gradually increase your rates.
    b. **Introductory Offers**: Consider offering introductory discounts or limited-time promotions to attract new clients.

Offering AI-Enhanced Services as Premium Options

1. **Define Premium Services**:
    a. **Advanced Features**: Identify features that set your premium services apart. This could include faster delivery times, in-depth research, comprehensive revisions, or exclusive use of advanced AI tools.
    b. **Customization**: Offer more personalized and tailored services in your premium packages. For example, customized content strategies, detailed analytics reports, or bespoke writing styles.
2. **Pricing Strategy**:
    a. **Higher Rates**: Set higher rates for premium services to reflect the additional value provided. Ensure that the pricing difference is justified by the enhanced features and benefits.
    b. **Upselling**: Use upselling techniques to encourage clients to choose premium packages. Highlight the added value and potential return on investment (ROI) of your premium services.
3. **Communicating Value**:
    a. **Detailed Descriptions**: Clearly describe the unique benefits of your premium services in your gig listings. Use bullet points and comparisons to emphasize the differences between standard and premium options.
    b. **Client Testimonials**: Include testimonials from clients who have used your premium services. Positive feedback and success stories can persuade potential clients to invest in higher-tier packages.

By effectively setting up your profiles, optimizing your gig listings, and strategically pricing your services, you can attract more clients and build a successful freelance business on Fiverr and Upwork. Highlighting your AI expertise and offering premium options will further enhance your competitiveness and appeal to a broader client base.

Chapter 5: Delivering High-Quality AI-Enhanced Services

Client Communication and Expectations

Managing Client Expectations about AI

1. **Educating Clients**:
    a. **Explain AI Capabilities**: Clearly explain what AI can and cannot do. Highlight that while AI can significantly enhance efficiency and accuracy, it still requires human oversight and creativity.
    b. **Set Realistic Expectations**: Manage expectations by explaining that AI-generated content might need refinement and customization to meet specific needs and standards.
2. **Transparency**:
    a. **Be Honest About AI Involvement**: Clearly state the extent to which AI will be used in the project. Transparency builds trust and sets realistic expectations for the final output.
    b. **Clarify Limitations**: Discuss potential limitations of AI, such as difficulties with nuanced language or highly creative tasks. Make sure clients understand that AI is a tool, not a replacement for human expertise.
3. **Define Deliverables**:
    a. **Detailed Project Scope**: Provide a detailed scope of the project, including what will be delivered, timelines, and the role of AI in each phase. This helps clients understand the process and anticipate the outcomes.
    b. **Milestones and Reviews**: Set clear milestones and review points. This allows for adjustments based on client feedback and ensures the project stays on track.

Effective Communication Strategies

1. **Initial Consultation**:
    a. **Understand Client Needs**: Start with a thorough consultation to understand the client's goals, target audience, and specific requirements. Use this information to tailor your AI-enhanced services accordingly.

b. **Demonstrate Expertise**: Share examples of previous AI-enhanced projects and explain how AI added value. This builds confidence in your skills and the technology.
2. **Regular Updates**:
   a. **Frequent Communication**: Keep clients updated on project progress through regular emails, calls, or video conferences. Transparency about progress and challenges builds trust.
   b. **Share Drafts and Samples**: Provide drafts or samples of AI-generated content at different stages. This allows clients to provide feedback and make necessary adjustments early in the process.
3. **Feedback and Revisions**:
   a. **Encourage Feedback**: Create an open environment where clients feel comfortable giving feedback. This ensures the final product meets their expectations.
   b. **Flexible Revisions**: Be open to making revisions based on client feedback. Highlight how AI can quickly adapt and make changes to meet evolving requirements.

Creating AI-Enhanced Content

Steps for Producing High-Quality AI-Generated Content

1. **Initial Setup**:
   a. **Define Objectives**: Clearly define the objectives of the content. Understand the purpose, target audience, and key messages that need to be conveyed.
   b. **Select AI Tools**: Choose the appropriate AI tools based on the project requirements. For example, use Jasper for content generation, Grammarly for grammar checks, and Copy.ai for marketing copy.
2. **Content Generation**:
   a. **Provide Detailed Prompts**: Input detailed and specific prompts into the AI tools. The more context and information you provide, the better the AI output will be.
   b. **Generate Multiple Versions**: Create multiple versions of the content using different prompts and angles. This provides options and allows for selecting the best version.
3. **Review and Refine**:
   a. **Initial Review**: Perform an initial review of the AI-generated content. Check for accuracy, relevance, and alignment with the project objectives.

b. **Human Touch**: Add a human touch to the content by refining language, adding personal insights, and ensuring it resonates with the target audience. Human creativity and intuition are crucial for high-quality content.

Quality Control and Human Touch

1. **Editing and Proofreading**:
   a. **Use AI Editing Tools**: Run the content through AI editing tools like Grammarly and ProWritingAid to catch grammar errors, style issues, and readability problems.
   b. **Human Review**: Conduct a thorough human review to ensure the content is polished and professional. Pay attention to nuances, tone, and flow that AI might miss.
2. **Consistency and Coherence**:
   a. **Maintain Consistency**: Ensure the content is consistent in tone, style, and messaging. This is especially important for larger projects with multiple pieces of content.
   b. **Check Coherence**: Verify that the content is coherent and logically structured. AI can sometimes produce disjointed text, so ensure the final product flows smoothly.
3. **Client Approval**:
   a. **Present Final Draft**: Present the final draft to the client for approval. Highlight the key elements and how AI was used to enhance the content.
   b. **Make Final Adjustments**: Be open to making final adjustments based on client feedback. Ensure the content meets their expectations and project requirements.
4. **Continuous Improvement**:
   a. **Gather Feedback**: After project completion, gather feedback from clients about the quality of the AI-enhanced content and the overall process.
   b. **Iterate and Improve**: Use this feedback to improve your use of AI tools and refine your content creation process for future projects.

By effectively managing client expectations, maintaining clear communication, and combining AI capabilities with human creativity, you can deliver high-quality AI-enhanced services that meet and exceed client expectations.

Chapter 6: Marketing and Growing Your Freelance Business

Building a Personal Brand

Developing a Unique Selling Proposition (USP)

1. **Identify Your Strengths**:
   a. **Assess Your Skills**: List out your skills, experiences, and what makes your services unique. Consider how your AI expertise sets you apart from other freelancers.
   b. **Client Needs**: Understand the common pain points and needs of your target clients. How can you solve their problems better or more efficiently than others?
2. **Craft Your USP**:
   a. **Be Specific**: Your USP should clearly articulate the unique benefits clients will receive from working with you. For example, "Providing cutting-edge AI-driven content solutions that enhance engagement and drive results."
   b. **Value Proposition**: Highlight the value you bring to clients, such as improved efficiency, higher quality content, or innovative approaches.
3. **Test and Refine**:
   a. **Gather Feedback**: Test your USP with existing clients or through surveys. Ask for feedback on how compelling and clear it is.
   b. **Refine Accordingly**: Use the feedback to refine your USP, making it stronger and more aligned with client needs.

Leveraging Social Media to Promote Your Services

1. **Choose the Right Platforms**:
   a. **Identify Where Your Clients Are**: Focus on platforms where your potential clients are most active. LinkedIn is great for professional networking, while Twitter and Instagram can be useful for showcasing work and engaging with a broader audience.
   b. **Consistency Across Platforms**: Maintain a consistent presence and message across all platforms to strengthen your brand.
2. **Create Valuable Content**:

a. **Educational Posts**: Share content that educates your audience about the benefits of AI in content creation. Blog posts, infographics, and videos explaining AI trends and tools can position you as an expert.
   b. **Showcase Your Work**: Post examples of your AI-enhanced projects, case studies, and client testimonials. Visual content like before-and-after comparisons can be particularly compelling.
3. **Engage with Your Audience**:
   a. **Respond to Comments**: Engage with followers by responding to comments and messages. Building a community around your brand fosters loyalty and trust.
   b. **Participate in Discussions**: Join relevant groups and discussions, sharing insights and advice. This can increase your visibility and establish you as a thought leader.

Networking and Building Relationships

Connecting with Other Freelancers and Potential Clients

1. **Join Professional Communities**:
   a. **Online Forums and Groups**: Participate in online forums and social media groups related to freelancing, AI, and your specific niche. Platforms like Reddit, Facebook, and LinkedIn have numerous groups where professionals exchange ideas and opportunities.
   b. **Freelancer Networks**: Join networks and platforms dedicated to freelancers, such as Upwork Community, Fiverr Forums, and Freelancer.com Groups.
2. **Attend Industry Events**:
   a. **Conferences and Webinars**: Attend (or virtually attend) industry conferences, webinars, and meetups. These events are great for learning about new trends and connecting with potential clients and collaborators.
   b. **Networking Events**: Participate in networking events specific to your industry. These provide opportunities to meet other professionals, exchange ideas, and form partnerships.
3. **Collaborate and Partner**:
   a. **Collaborative Projects**: Partner with other freelancers on larger projects. This can help you gain experience, expand your network, and take on more significant projects.
   b. **Cross-Promotions**: Collaborate on cross-promotions with other freelancers or small businesses. For instance, a graphic designer and a content writer could offer joint services.

Building a Strong Client Base

1. **Deliver Exceptional Service**:
   a. **Quality Work**: Consistently deliver high-quality work that meets or exceeds client expectations. Quality service leads to repeat business and referrals.
   b. **Customer Service**: Be responsive and communicative. Address any issues promptly and professionally to maintain strong client relationships.
2. **Ask for Referrals and Reviews**:
   a. **Client Testimonials**: Request testimonials from satisfied clients. Display these prominently on your website and profiles to build credibility.
   b. **Referral Programs**: Implement a referral program where existing clients receive discounts or bonuses for referring new clients to you.
3. **Maintain Relationships**:
   a. **Follow-Up**: Regularly check in with past clients. Update them on new services or tools you're offering and show appreciation for their business.
   b. **Personal Touches**: Send personalized thank-you notes, holiday greetings, or small tokens of appreciation to strengthen client relationships.

Scaling Your Business

Offering Additional Services

1. **Identify Client Needs**:
   a. **Analyze Demand**: Identify additional services that complement your existing offerings. For instance, if you provide AI-powered content creation, you might also offer SEO optimization, social media management, or data analytics.
   b. **Client Feedback**: Gather feedback from clients to understand their additional needs and preferences.
2. **Expand Your Skill Set**:
   a. **Continuous Learning**: Invest in continuous learning to expand your skill set. Online courses, workshops, and certifications can help you offer new services.
   b. **Experiment and Innovate**: Experiment with new tools and techniques to innovate and offer cutting-edge services to clients.
3. **Package Services**:

a. **Service Bundles**: Create service bundles that provide comprehensive solutions. For example, a content creation package could include writing, editing, SEO, and social media promotion.
   b. **Tiered Offerings**: Offer tiered service levels (basic, standard, premium) to cater to different client budgets and needs.

Hiring Virtual Assistants and Subcontractors

1. **Define Roles and Tasks**:
   a. **Identify Tasks**: List out tasks that can be delegated, such as administrative work, research, or specific aspects of content creation.
   b. **Clear Job Descriptions**: Create clear job descriptions for virtual assistants or subcontractors. Define their roles, responsibilities, and expectations.
2. **Find the Right Talent**:
   a. **Freelance Platforms**: Use platforms like Upwork, Fiverr, or specialized VA agencies to find qualified virtual assistants or subcontractors.
   b. **Screening and Interviews**: Screen candidates thoroughly and conduct interviews to ensure they have the necessary skills and fit your business culture.
3. **Onboarding and Training**:
   a. **Comprehensive Onboarding**: Provide comprehensive onboarding to familiarize new hires with your business processes, tools, and expectations.
   b. **Ongoing Training**: Offer ongoing training and support to ensure your team is up-to-date with the latest tools and techniques.
4. **Effective Management**:
   a. **Communication Tools**: Use communication and project management tools like Slack, Trello, or Asana to manage your team and projects effectively.
   b. **Regular Check-Ins**: Schedule regular check-ins and progress reviews to ensure tasks are on track and any issues are addressed promptly.

By building a strong personal brand, effectively using social media, networking, and scaling your business strategically, you can grow your freelance business and achieve long-term success.

Chapter 7: Overcoming Challenges and Staying Competitive

Common Challenges in Freelancing with AI

Ethical Considerations

1. **Bias and Fairness**:
    a. **Understanding AI Bias**: AI tools can inadvertently perpetuate biases present in training data. It's crucial to recognize how biases might impact your content and take steps to mitigate them.
    b. **Transparency**: Be transparent with clients about the limitations and potential biases of AI tools. Ensure your work strives for fairness and inclusivity.
2. **Data Privacy**:
    a. **Protecting Client Data**: Ensure that any data you handle, whether personal or sensitive, is protected. Use secure tools and platforms to manage client information and adhere to privacy regulations.
    b. **AI Data Usage**: Understand how AI tools use and store data. Avoid using tools that may misuse or improperly store sensitive client information.
3. **Intellectual Property**:
    a. **Originality of AI-Generated Content**: Ensure that AI-generated content does not inadvertently infringe on intellectual property rights. Verify that the content is original and properly attributed.
    b. **Client Agreements**: Clearly define intellectual property rights in client agreements, specifying who owns the rights to AI-generated content.

Staying Updated with AI Advancements

1. **Rapid Technological Changes**:
    a. **Monitor Industry News**: Stay informed about the latest developments in AI technology. Follow industry news sources, blogs, and thought leaders to keep up with advancements.
    b. **Join Professional Groups**: Engage with professional groups and forums focused on AI. Participate in discussions and stay updated on emerging trends and tools.
2. **Tool Updates and New Releases**:

a. **Regular Tool Reviews**: Regularly review and assess the tools you use. Ensure they are updated and check for new features or improvements.
   b. **Evaluate New Tools**: Experiment with new AI tools and platforms. Evaluate their effectiveness and determine if they can enhance your services or streamline your workflow.

Continuous Learning and Improvement

Keeping Your Skills and Tools Up to Date

1. **Ongoing Skill Development**:
   a. **Identify Skill Gaps**: Regularly assess your skills and identify areas for improvement. Focus on both AI-specific skills and broader freelancing skills.
   b. **Advanced Training**: Seek out advanced training opportunities to deepen your expertise in AI. Consider certifications, specialized courses, and workshops.
2. **Tool Proficiency**:
   a. **Stay Proficient**: Maintain proficiency with the AI tools you use. Explore new features, updates, and best practices to maximize their effectiveness.
   b. **Experiment and Innovate**: Experiment with new tools and technologies. Be open to incorporating innovative solutions into your workflow.

Investing in Ongoing Education and Training

1. **Educational Resources**:
   a. **Online Courses and Certifications**: Invest in online courses and certifications related to AI and content creation. Platforms like Coursera, Udemy, and LinkedIn Learning offer valuable resources.
   b. **Workshops and Webinars**: Attend workshops and webinars to learn from industry experts. These events often provide insights into cutting-edge practices and technologies.
2. **Professional Development**:
   a. **Industry Conferences**: Attend industry conferences and events. These gatherings offer opportunities to learn from leaders, network with peers, and stay informed about trends.

b. **Books and Journals**: Read books and academic journals on AI and freelancing. Staying informed through various media can provide new perspectives and ideas.
3. **Peer Learning and Networking**:
   a. **Join Study Groups**: Join or form study groups with other professionals in your field. Collaborative learning can enhance your skills and provide support.
   b. **Mentorship**: Seek out mentors or offer mentorship to others. Mentoring relationships can provide valuable insights and help you stay competitive.

By addressing ethical considerations, staying updated with AI advancements, and investing in continuous learning, you can overcome challenges and maintain a competitive edge in the freelancing market. Embracing a proactive approach to skill development and industry trends will ensure that you remain relevant and successful in the evolving landscape of AI-driven freelancing.

Chapter 8: Future Trends in Freelancing with AI

Emerging AI Technologies

New AI Tools on the Horizon

1. **Advanced Natural Language Processing (NLP)**:
   a. **Enhanced Text Generation**: Future NLP models will be more adept at generating human-like text with improved context understanding and creativity. These tools will offer more sophisticated options for content creation, making them invaluable for freelancers involved in writing and editing.
   b. **Contextual Understanding**: Emerging NLP tools will better understand and retain context across longer pieces of text, reducing the need for extensive human editing and making AI-generated content more coherent and engaging.
2. **AI-Powered Creativity Tools**:
   a. **Creative Assistance**: New AI tools will assist in creative processes such as ideation, brainstorming, and design. These tools will help freelancers in creative fields generate innovative concepts and streamline their creative workflows.
   b. **Visual Content Generation**: Advancements in AI will enable the creation of high-quality visuals and graphics with minimal input. Tools like DALL-E and Midjourney are paving the way for more sophisticated visual content generation.
3. **AI for Personalization**:
   a. **Customized Content**: Future AI tools will offer advanced personalization capabilities, enabling freelancers to create highly tailored content based on individual client preferences and audience data.
   b. **Adaptive Learning**: AI will increasingly adapt to user preferences and behaviors, allowing for more personalized and relevant content delivery.
4. **AI in Project Management and Automation**:
   a. **Automated Workflow Management**: AI tools will enhance project management by automating routine tasks, scheduling, and task delegation. This will help freelancers manage multiple projects more efficiently and focus on high-value activities.

b. **Predictive Analytics**: Future AI tools will use predictive analytics to anticipate project needs, optimize resource allocation, and improve decision-making.

How These Technologies Will Impact Freelancing

1. **Increased Efficiency and Productivity**:
    a. **Streamlined Processes**: Advanced AI tools will automate repetitive tasks and streamline workflows, allowing freelancers to work more efficiently and handle a higher volume of work.
    b. **Time Savings**: By reducing the time spent on routine tasks, freelancers can focus on strategic and creative aspects of their work, leading to increased productivity and output.
2. **Enhanced Quality of Work**:
    a. **Improved Accuracy**: New AI tools will offer higher accuracy in tasks such as content generation, editing, and data analysis, resulting in higher quality deliverables.
    b. **Creative Innovation**: AI-powered creativity tools will enable freelancers to explore new creative avenues and deliver innovative solutions to clients.
3. **New Opportunities and Niches**:
    a. **Emerging Fields**: The development of new AI technologies will create new freelancing opportunities and niches. Freelancers will need to stay updated on these trends to capitalize on emerging markets.
    b. **Specialized Expertise**: As AI tools become more advanced, there will be a growing demand for freelancers with specialized expertise in these technologies, creating new avenues for career growth.

Preparing for the Future

Adapting to Changes in the Market

1. **Continuous Learning and Skill Development**:
    a. **Stay Informed**: Regularly update your knowledge on emerging AI technologies and market trends. Follow industry news, attend webinars, and engage in continuous education to stay ahead.
    b. **Skill Diversification**: Expand your skill set to include new AI tools and technologies. Diversifying your skills will make you more adaptable to changing market demands and increase your competitiveness.
2. **Flexibility and Agility**:

a. **Embrace Change**: Be open to adopting new tools and methodologies as they become available. Flexibility will help you stay relevant and quickly adapt to market shifts.
   b. **Agile Approach**: Implement an agile approach to your freelance business. This includes being responsive to client feedback, experimenting with new tools, and adjusting your services based on market trends.
3. **Networking and Collaboration**:
   a. **Build Connections**: Network with other professionals and industry experts to stay informed about the latest developments and opportunities. Collaborate with peers to explore new ideas and technologies.
   b. **Partnerships**: Form strategic partnerships with other freelancers or businesses to leverage complementary skills and stay competitive in the evolving market.

Future-Proofing Your Freelance Business

1. **Invest in Technology**:
   a. **Adopt New Tools**: Invest in the latest AI tools and technologies that can enhance your services and improve efficiency. Early adoption can give you a competitive edge and keep your business relevant.
   b. **Upgrade Infrastructure**: Ensure your technology infrastructure is up-to-date and capable of supporting new tools and workflows. This includes investing in hardware, software, and security measures.
2. **Develop a Strong Online Presence**:
   a. **Personal Branding**: Strengthen your personal brand and online presence to stand out in a competitive market. Use social media, content marketing, and a professional website to showcase your expertise and attract clients.
   b. **Thought Leadership**: Position yourself as a thought leader by sharing insights, writing articles, and participating in industry discussions. This will help you stay visible and relevant in your field.
3. **Build a Resilient Business Model**:
   a. **Diversify Income Streams**: Explore multiple income streams to reduce reliance on a single source of revenue. This could include offering different services, creating digital products, or leveraging passive income opportunities.
   b. **Client Relationships**: Focus on building long-term relationships with clients by delivering exceptional service and adding value. Strong

client relationships can provide stability and opportunities for repeat business.

By staying informed about emerging AI technologies, adapting to market changes, and proactively preparing for the future, you can ensure that your freelance business remains competitive and resilient in the evolving landscape of AI-driven freelancing. Embracing continuous learning and innovation will position you for long-term success and growth.

Conclusion

Recap of Key Points

1. **Understanding AI in Content Creation**:
   a. AI has revolutionized content creation by enhancing efficiency and precision. Tools such as advanced NLP models and creative assistance platforms enable freelancers to produce high-quality content with ease.
   b. Key AI tools for writing, editing, and content management streamline workflows and improve productivity, allowing freelancers to focus on strategic and creative aspects of their work.
2. **Setting Up Your Freelance Business**:
   a. Choosing a niche that aligns with your skills and market demand is crucial for success. Building a portfolio that showcases your AI-enhanced work and establishing a professional online presence are essential steps in attracting clients.
   b. Effective profile creation and optimization on platforms like Fiverr and Upwork help in establishing a strong foothold in the freelance market.
3. **Essential AI Tools for Freelancers**:
   a. Leveraging AI writing, editing, and content creation tools can significantly enhance the quality and efficiency of your work. Integrating these tools into your workflow allows for better management of repetitive tasks and streamlined content generation.
4. **Delivering High-Quality AI-Enhanced Services**:
   a. Managing client expectations, maintaining clear communication, and combining AI capabilities with human creativity are key to delivering exceptional services. Regularly refining and reviewing AI-generated content ensures it meets client standards.
5. **Marketing and Growing Your Freelance Business**:
   a. Building a personal brand, leveraging social media, and networking are critical for promoting your services and expanding your client base. Scaling your business through additional services and hiring support staff can further enhance your growth potential.
6. **Overcoming Challenges and Staying Competitive**:
   a. Addressing ethical considerations, staying updated with AI advancements, and investing in continuous learning are essential for overcoming challenges and maintaining a competitive edge. Embracing new technologies and adapting to market changes will help future-proof your business.
7. **Future Trends in Freelancing with AI**:

a. Emerging AI technologies, such as advanced NLP models and AI-powered creativity tools, will continue to impact the freelancing landscape. Staying informed about these trends and preparing for future changes will ensure you remain relevant and successful in the evolving market.

Encouragement and Final Thoughts

1. **Embrace the AI Revolution**:
    a. The integration of AI into freelancing offers unparalleled opportunities for innovation and efficiency. Embrace the advancements and leverage them to enhance your services, streamline your processes, and deliver exceptional value to your clients.
2. **Pursue Continuous Growth**:
    a. The world of freelancing and AI is dynamic and ever-changing. Commit to continuous learning and skill development to stay ahead of the curve. Seek out new knowledge, experiment with emerging tools, and refine your expertise to remain competitive and successful.
3. **Foster a Passion for Creativity and Excellence**:
    a. AI is a powerful tool, but it's your creativity, expertise, and dedication that will truly set you apart. Strive for excellence in every project and let your passion for your craft shine through in your work. Your unique perspective and commitment to quality will make a significant impact.
4. **Stay Resilient and Adaptable**:
    a. Freelancing can be challenging, and the integration of AI adds another layer of complexity. Stay resilient in the face of challenges and be adaptable to change. Your ability to navigate the evolving landscape with agility and confidence will be key to your long-term success.
5. **Inspire and Lead**:
    a. As an AI-powered freelancer, you have the opportunity to lead and inspire others in the industry. Share your experiences, mentor others, and contribute to the growth and advancement of the freelancing community.

Remember, the future of freelancing with AI is bright and full of possibilities. Embrace the journey with enthusiasm and determination, and you'll find success and fulfillment in this exciting and transformative field. Your innovation, adaptability, and passion will drive your success as you continue to shape the future of freelancing with AI.

Resources and Appendices

List of Recommended AI Tools

Writing Tools

1. **Jasper (formerly Jarvis)**
   a. **Description**: Jasper is a powerful AI writing assistant that helps generate high-quality content for various purposes, including blog posts, marketing copy, and social media updates. It offers a variety of templates and a user-friendly interface to streamline your content creation process.
2. **Grammarly**
   a. **Description**: Grammarly provides advanced grammar and spell-checking, style suggestions, and plagiarism detection. It is an essential tool for ensuring your content is polished, error-free, and professionally written.
3. **Copy.ai**
   a. **Description**: Copy.ai leverages AI to generate marketing copy, social media posts, and product descriptions. It offers various templates and creative prompts to help you produce engaging content efficiently.

Editing and Proofreading Tools

1. **Hemingway Editor**
   a. **Description**: The Hemingway Editor is designed to improve the clarity and readability of your writing. It highlights complex sentences, passive voice, and other issues to help you craft concise and effective content.
2. **ProWritingAid**
   a. **Description**: ProWritingAid provides in-depth reports on grammar, style, and readability. This tool offers detailed suggestions and corrections to enhance the quality of your writing.

Content Creation and Management Tools

1. **Surfer SEO**
   a. **Description**: Surfer SEO assists in optimizing content for search engines by providing insights into keyword usage, content structure,

and competitive analysis. It helps you improve your content's visibility and ranking.
2. **ContentBot**
   a. **Description**: ContentBot is an AI tool for generating blog posts, articles, and marketing copy. It includes a range of content templates and customization options to suit various writing needs.
3. **BuzzSumo**
   a. **Description**: BuzzSumo is a content research and analysis tool that helps identify trending topics and high-performing content. It supports content ideation and competitive research.

Further Reading

Books

1. **"Artificial Intelligence: A Guide for Thinking Humans" by Melanie Mitchell**
   a. **Description**: This book provides a comprehensive overview of AI, its capabilities, and its implications for society. It offers valuable insights into the current state of AI and its future potential.
2. **"AI Superpowers: China, Silicon Valley, and the New World Order" by Kai-Fu Lee**
   a. **Description**: This book explores the global impact of AI, comparing developments in China and Silicon Valley. It provides context on how AI is transforming industries and economies.

Articles

1. **"The Future of AI: Opportunities and Challenges"**
   a. **Description**: This article discusses emerging trends and future possibilities in AI technology, covering both potential benefits and challenges.
2. **"How AI is Transforming Freelancing"**
   a. **Description**: A detailed analysis of how AI tools are reshaping the freelancing landscape, including practical examples and case studies.

Courses

1. **"AI For Everyone" by Andrew Ng**
   a. **Description**: A beginner-friendly course that provides an overview of AI and its applications across various industries. It's ideal for understanding AI's potential impact on your work.

2. **"Freelancing on Fiverr: Your Guide to Success"**
    a. **Description**: This course offers guidance on succeeding on Fiverr, covering profile setup, gig creation, and strategies for attracting clients.

Templates and Worksheets

While specific templates and worksheets are not included, consider creating or sourcing the following to support your freelance business:

1. **Portfolio Template**: A customizable portfolio to showcase your AI-enhanced work, including case studies and project examples.
2. **Client Communication Templates**: Professional templates for proposals, contracts, and client feedback forms to streamline communication and project management.
3. **Pricing Worksheets**: Worksheets to calculate your rates, budget, and manage your freelance finances effectively.

These resources will help you navigate the world of freelancing with AI, providing practical support and guidance as you build and grow your business.

Creating "Freelancing with AI" has been a deeply fulfilling journey, and I am grateful for the opportunity to share my knowledge and experiences with you.

First and foremost, I would like to thank all the readers and freelancers who have inspired me to explore the integration of AI in the freelancing world. Your curiosity and drive to innovate have been a constant source of motivation for me.

This book is the result of countless hours of research, writing, and revision. I appreciate the support and understanding of everyone who has been part of my journey, allowing me the time and space to bring this project to life.

I am also grateful for the advancements in technology that have made freelancing with AI a viable and exciting option for so many. The tools and platforms available today are truly remarkable, and I am excited to see how they will continue to evolve.

Lastly, I would like to extend my heartfelt thanks to you, the reader. Your interest in "Freelancing with AI" is the ultimate reward for my efforts. I hope this book provides you with valuable insights and practical guidance on your freelancing journey.

With sincere appreciation,

Rakesh Chittineni

www.ingramcontent.com/pod-product-compliance
Lightning Source LLC
Chambersburg PA
CBHW072055230526

45479CB00010B/1087